LET'S PLAY SPORTS!

HOCKEY

by Tessa Kenan

TABLE OF CONTENTS

Words to Know.............2

Let's Play Hockey!.............3

Let's Review!.............16

Index.............16

WORDS TO KNOW

goalie

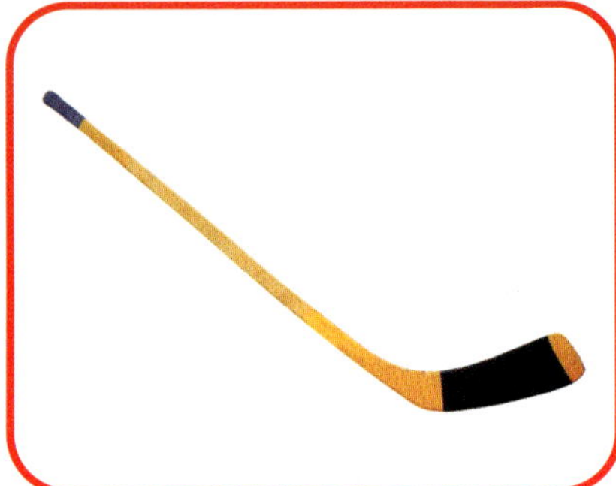
hockey stick

ice rink

net

puck

skates

LET'S PLAY HOCKEY!

Let's go to the ice rink!

hockey
skate

She puts on skates.

We skate on the ice.

He hits the puck.

He uses a hockey stick.

She guards the net.

She is the goalie.

He shoots!

She stops the puck!

No goal!

LET'S REVIEW!

Point to the equipment below that is needed to play hockey.

INDEX

goal 15
goalie 11
hockey stick 9
ice rink 3
net 10
puck 8, 14
shoots 13
skates 5